The Tear of an Orphan Child

Poems

Mwana Fombe

Mwanaka Media and Publishing Pvt Ltd,
Chitungwiza Zimbabwe
*

Creativity, Wisdom and Beauty

Publisher: *Mmap*

Mwanaka Media and Publishing Pvt Ltd

24 Svosve Road, Zengeza 1

Chitungwiza Zimbabwe

mwanaka@yahoo.com

mwanaka13@gmail.com

www.africanbookscollective.com/publishers/mwanaka-media-and-publishing

https://facebook.com/MwanakaMediaAndPublishing/

Distributed in and outside N. America by African Books Collective

orders@africanbookscollective.com

www.africanbookscollective.com

ISBN: 978-1-77928-412-9

EAN: 9781779284129

© Mwana Fombe 2025

All rights reserved.

No part of this book may be reproduced or transmitted in any form or by any means, mechanical or electronic, including photocopying and recording, or be stored in any information storage or retrieval system, without written permission from the publisher

DISCLAIMER

All views expressed in this publication are those of the author and do not necessarily reflect the views of *Mmap*.

To my dear son Travis, who learned from a very early age to deal with the hardships of life that I love and owe him very much.

Contents

Intoduction

My exhausted fingers

Teacher

The unseen book

Avozinha "Maria"

Mom Africa

The poem of love, that killed Rabeca

I'm taking, My way

Which verses are these?

The tear, Of an orphan child

The secret, Of Care for Life

When love kills, The kid heart

Funguayi

The tiger look

My son travis

On sunshine

Helping and giving

looking for an answer

The future

About an uncertain poem

The stolen love

The date of my days

Crying of silence

despair of love

Gone away "Mavungatinta

the waste

Fear of your verses

Dad

the treacherous

The past

Joy of instincts

May be one day

Life is too short

Confused

Nothing to complain

Sad verse

Is for you baby

Distant world

Poetry world

The walls Of love

Love

Mercy of love

Heart ablaze

Matter of love

The other side of the love

Where's love

Introduction

The collection of these poems reflect in me moments of joy and sadness that suffocated my poetic life.

Writing poems in English is a greatest challenge particularly here in Mozambique where the numbers of readers are limited and English is not our official language.

The poem mom Africa, was published in a film of *Care for Life in United States* in 2004 with many others poems.

I can honestly say that the short time that I have spent writing has changed the course of the rest of my life and now I have a nose not to smell the flowers but to smell the flavour of being a poet. I feel that I see the world now through I clearer lens than I had in the past.

Clarity has always been a coveted commodity for me.

When I started writing poetry, first it was due to love frustrations, I liked to be alone to get rid of my demons that tortured me every day. The desire to be alone, writing, was a kind of therapy, to find a cure for the divorce, as well to find my poetic voice to the world, that voice that lives in me that transcends from life to paper.

My exhausted fingers

My fingers are completely exhausted
Because of thinking in open air
In a vague world, in wild's life
They are tired because of seeing
And the understandable dynamic way
They are in criticizing others
The gun to combat the wild boars
My fingers are totally dead
Of touching the world in a line
In one idea, in one thought
These fingers are professionally logic
However, sometimes they don't seem creature
But as generous a bird
When it is building it's net

But sometimes seem like poison
Because they see what others
Blindly live to see
But I am afraid of them
Because when it's cool
They groan and cry
But when wild boars devour things
And never feed up
My exhausted fingers

September 2001

Teacher

Teacher doesn't wear pugnacity
To write on a hard wood
Doesn't shout to a deaf stone
For it to purples itself
Is intellectually anxious
He takes out the stains
To think clearly and concisely
Reflect, criticizes the practice
For an ideological education
Doesn't show his guitar deaf
 Proof to be a singer
The branch of mixed knowledge
Is not hidden in the moon
Teacher, is a logic thinker
Who's thirsty of methodical rigorist?

Ethic, aesthetics is his cup of tea
The lesson plan is not taboo
He's always hungry in knowledge
And Never fed up
But the teacher because of 12 October, no!
Is not happy when receiving gift?
Without nose to smell flowers
With an ear to hear piano
With a head to wear cup
With a strong hand to bit students
With a long neck to keep an eye on
When the students are writing tests
Impermeable in change, resistant
Teaches without pedagogical competences
Teacher who behaves like a soldier
Teacher who is very traditional?
Who waits for any litle reward?
Without sacrifice

Isn't necessary to offer gift
But a serious teacher deserves rewards
Of all the time...

12 October 2004

The unseen book

The book was totally defaulted

Due to the blowing of wind

The page's skim through

He gave an objective and tender look

But read nothing between lines

The letters were so dark like

A midnight with heavenly rain

The wind blew again

The hurricane rolled

He curiously looked

But a crossed line he saw

The tears rained on the face

In intention of washing his eyes

His sick head complains

Because the eyes were very hungry

And wanted to see the edition

The hurricane rolled and rolled

But this time the book was closed

He cried and cried and cried

The way of washing his eyes

A mentally unstable man

The book wasn't available

Suddenly the rain came

It was raining cats and dogs

He gave an askance look

But he saw nothing

The hurricane yelled

The man disappeared...

December 2000

Avozinha "Maria"

I decided to say something true
I joined my true fingers
To say no or yes darling
I perfumed the paper
So that you measure my love
I drew the letter
So that you may make assessment
I enclosed my handsome picture
So that you 'll not hesitate
The love I'm looking for
I joined my feelings to answer
Your intellectual questions
I'm nothing in this world
I'm man who loves himself
Whose love hasn't frontiers

Who loves like bees how they

Love the flowers

I'm really a fish immerged

Into the salty water

In the morning I think

In the evening I dream being

With your image

My heart has uncountable wounds

Because of thinking about you

My blood is very mixed

With strong emotions

That define the man that I'm today

I am your fuel

My unforgettable

17 December 2000

Mom Africa

Due to your existence
We'll never be forgotten
I was half crazy of course
When you were sick

Many of your children
They've never seen you
Because they were still children
When they were taken from you

I've overheard news of your life
But I don't know, where are you?
I know that you've been suffering
Several operations in your body

I would like to come to you

To remember the laughter, you heard
The lullabies I deeply had
The tears you wiped
I'm conscious that you're suffering
War, poverty, flood, starvation
Are destroying everyday your children

But where are you mom?
I send my friend "Care For Life"
To alleviate your suffering
To promote self-reliance

To instill hope in your mom   I
hope my friend Care For Life
Will take care of you
I know that you're old enough
You need someone to care for your life

Mom!

November 10, 2001

The poem of love that killed Rabeca

After a lemonade,

I wrote a poem to Rebecca,

Replying to her blinding and lovely letter

In the first little words,

I pasted a banana's chocolate,

She quickly savoured,

And ate with all love

In following lines, I wrote,

Words animate

Words blessed

Words powerful

Words romantics

Words of life

Words sweets

Words extremely loved
Like a given flower
A true terrorism of love
In the last stanza
I pasted a mirror,
She looked daggers at it,
She looked and laughed
She happily drank the poem
And became intoxicated of love
She suddenly broke the mirror
She cried and cried and cried of emotions
Unfortunately, by love was killed

November 10, 2004

I'm taking my way

I'm taking my way
My way I take to somewhere
To touch the feeling of hay
For a bright future

I'm taking my skills
To cast them into the sea
Where my heart lives
And plays opera

You could be mine
But I made up my mind
To drop to you a serious line
In silent words, you'll remind

I'll never again lay
On your forgetful arms
In kind, I won't repay
Because I'll be in a fortress

Your unchangeable behaviour
Hour, succumbed I stayed
I'll look for saviour
To quench the fire, I survived

I'll drop you a line
In useless words uttered
You'll blindly understand
The aim of this prose

November 14, 2003

Which verses are these?

These are verses that I cooked

Without onions and tomatoes

To taste

There are too sour due to the vinegar

The salt is in excess

Pepper is missing

But which verses are these?

Readers have never seen

Verses that cry out

So many idioms

Idioms recycled in a language

Sometimes confounded

Transitively lives some one

A master who knows interior

Who can write in hungry tone?

But which verses are these?
Are sprouting into poet's brain
Sometimes sour too
Sometimes too sweet
Sometimes affectionate
Sometimes bitter
Which verses are these?

November 10, 2003

The tear of an orphan child

I saw an orphan crying

I asked to buy her tears

she gave me them for free

I put in a glass cup

It was similar to water

Suddenly the colour changed

I became blind

So I wore eyeglasses to see

I started seeing the glass cup

But it was neither tear nor water

Just some words like "carry-me to you"

"Give me hope" and "I need a shelter"

I tasted the tears

They were so bitter, so sour

I heard his sad laughter

And we cried together...

The secret of Care For Life

Care For Life starts with care

And ends with life

Who can tell me?

 the secret of this name

Who can spell it to me

Who can guess the meaning?

Who can see the hope?

Cindy has a sea in it

Blair has a bless in it

God has a check in it

Now tell me the secret of this name

Life has luck in it

For has fame in it

Care has a career in it

Now tell me

Who alleviates suffering?

Who promotes self-reliance?

Who instils hope in orphan?

Who wipes the baby tears?

Who hear the laughter?

Who says that change

Is possible?

Care For Life...

July 2003

When love kills kid heart

The heart beats

When the eyes cry out

The fear disappears

When the tired mouth complains

The state of mind opens

When love steals

The heart becomes sick

The magic love touches

During glorious mild sunny day

When hallucination appears

I become of course homesick

Due to the delicious smell of love

When the sense had been heightened

All wounds seem curable

But when my face cries

I feel the inevitable device
The brief life was absolutely
Idyllic
When the love stoned my heart
And I find it rather bizarre
I immediately become dumb
Like slackened baby's heart
(...)!

July 2000

Fungayi

All I wanted
It's what life gave -me
A beautiful and virtuous woman
in my loving arms

First, I cried with emotion
'Cause life smiled on me
In your eyes I found
The answers I was looking for

From distant lands came
I knew that one day I would
That day love would burn with strength
I saw the poetry of your beauty

Fungayi is my fuel
to walk with
Leaves Zimbabwe for Zimbabweans
In my heart it has a place

I love you like bees
 how they love the flowers
I put my trust in you
For the first time my heart leapt for joy
Of you in my hands, darling

June 6, 2022

The tiger look

But a look blesses
The love you want
The time you feel
The moment you like

The look deserves biter
And sweat life
Life of numerous problem
Life of biter look

A tiger look
Is a lion heart
With sure and uncertain

Wind of life

A lion and the fate
Is a look of disgraced river?
Where worms die of hunter
And fish die of thirsty

The life, the look
The dead blood
Cry for duty look....

November 2004

My son Travis

You were born in a moment
Of a good democracy
Moment that job is a paper and pencil
Moment that reading and writing

Is the blessed skills
Moment that a hug a lot
Was missing me
Moment of tranquillity, of course

Moment of disgrace
Born to this round world
Carrying a travel in it

Moment that kissing anyway

Is an option
Moment that beehive
Is a deadly weapon

Moment that everybody
Wants to be a winner
Moment of closed and
Opened society...

April, 11 2004

On sunshine

I wanted to walk away
On the adventure of sun
I beg down on my knees
Just a pleasure to walk away
To see the leg's pregnant
I cried on my knees
But I should of course
Understand the round world
I should understand
 The complexity of it
but nothing I bear
the sunshine show
the life, joy and disgrace
begging to the sky
to the crazy life

I beg and cried

For an intangible bright

I shut up the feelings

I open my hears

I felt the hair roaring

I hear the blood running

I saw the heart crying

But the way was shiny

And dark

The hungry tourist

Lost his way

On the mouth of destination

On the sunshine

September 2003

Helping and giving

Help can't take place if...
Love is insane and crazy
Money is a game of living

Is better to give than receiving
You can't laugh to the poverty

Because you are a part of it
You can cry to stop your vice
But your crying will not help

(...)

Looking for an answer

looking for the answer
Screams in unknown direction
I wish it was a bet
From a path never taken

trembling voices of people
Who screamed to just shut up
Others distinguished themselves crying promises
Which were never fulfilled to speak

Why are there so many questions?
That fate can't tell
There are some quotes in the background.

Where silence can mourn

I dislodged by the feeling of pity
I hate the joy of teeth
and I love the joy of the eyes
A brother accumulated by stress

Sit down and tune your gullible ear
Sad ear wanted to hear what I wanted to hear
Someone sent me once
could not accept it
But conform to hardness
forgive my intimacy
Despite killing myself I learned to forgive

The future

The promiscuous future
it's a promising adventure
because in it I retreat
to brush my predecessor

the truth is uncertainty
that a plan leads us
thoughts are like a courtesy
there is an imagination that I propose

the wait is a delay
to weave hope
so that certainty is lapse
a sometimes lapse of trust

Build the future from the past
For disaccrediting in cleverness
Sadness has passed me by
Feelings ruined by dexterity

the sum of truths
Sink into oblivion
Truths that are my pains
Who are forgiven in discounting?

8.14.2016

About an uncertain poem

In my thoughts I relapsed
Nightmare by me refused
With my hands tied on the floor I begged
The time! My reserved thought

Possible is a possibility
About the ultraviolent rays of me
So it warms up me to the nerves of identity
Others kneeling on the spirit of the ancestors

The crazy ones that are families and people
They were men of war and terror
My thoughts have seen enough sadness
When the danger of love approached

2022

The stolen love

you took my effort
Well I knew it was useful
Today leaves me in this frenzy
Immersed in the futile world

Look at your non-existent smile
I've hated myself for a long time
Who has the whys' and the non-existent man?
For in him you run over your thoughts

Today's love is a stir
That is issued just to occupy the time, no
Then discard yourself like a lost soul ,no

For other times of setback

I knew that the useful was useless
But now it's enough to know how to cry
For pain to be "useful"
That sometimes makes me blind

I know your beauty shines for me
But I'm nobody's

Crying is a scheme that cried

26.10.2015

The date of my days

until the date of my days
in a less forgotten sum
due to the accumulation of past sorrows
for having a lucid idea

the bitter past
it was like sleepy dreams
sometimes in silence I ask myself
how I supported with bizarre ideas

I, in the cult character
could float and sink to fate
because I'm from infinity

Until the date of my days

Today it's me, disenchanted by time

because nothing has changed in time

2018

Crying of silence

about the speech of the hidden silence
desire is hidden in sleep insomnia
rust of a cast iron
is the comparison that is left in the background

in miracles of the knees
could cry on the nose
to lessen the stray pain
in the sphere of that time

the sometimes forgotten guests
for the poverty that saw them being born, growing
how long can you calculate the pain of madmen
that look like people who love remorse
see people submerged at feet height

despair of love

when I feel weak
my pain follows my instinct
crying, I know very little
I've never called anyone
look makes me cry on the skin
the 'waters disorderly flow
over a sea that doesn't exist
the size that the pain carries
thermometers cost the price of love
a little takes the feeling
to the steps of time, forget
silent screams that never existed
were after all of an eternal man
words sensing in secrets
run against time

the will is captivated in desires

are priceless questions

for these things to love solitude

lives will never be in vain

madness in the ambush of time

to find a fragile void

2019

Gone away "Mavungatinta"

Why have you stopped; you rejoiced
Left your mouth in this turmoil
Outside the law reason; did you find
Laziness was yours therefore

No; I do not want
To breathe unbreathable air
Your taste is not integral
This being is yours; it's pitiful

Fake hugs are what they contain
Too many "mavungatinta" to have reason
Heart spell is from beyond

In the end! Darkness is thought

Grasshopper loses his mind when he breaks his wings

They are plucked from the ground; dies like a poor thing

December 19, 2019

4:50 minutes in the morning

*mavungatina -in sena language means messy girl

the waste

Living in bitterness from the same roof
It goes against nature; want conditions to live. Pains
 fall asleep in the chest
Scars of the past live

Assume a shameful loss; conditions
Pick wrong cards in this hellish world
Saturated by the debts of conditions
Play in the poor kid's arms

Walking on nobody's road
In a trick of the spirits emotions
Obsessed with no vision of this fear

There are drummers that play in love
In the silence of a dagger stare

Love without life or taste

December 24, 2019

Fear of your verses

hug me when
am scared
There's a world inside me
you will never see
Secrets I can't hide
Darkness is my fear
Thunder is my war
Assure me when I fall
Fix it when it's wrong
Don't kill me inside
when am dead?
love me when I'm gone
don't betray me when
am in dust
February 20, 2020

Dad

I threw wishes on the floor
consumed by nerves
All lived in vain
Today I cry verses

I found lost love
In the stubbornness of the carnal; wishes
Today seen as a bastard
I want your jewellery

You woke me up from the terrible pain
When I lost geography
From the road of love

I wet the verses
some real words

But denied the hugs

February 16, 2020

the treacherous

Treacherous is a friend

Hide hurts from his punishment

He Hugs to take advantages of you

He thinks, he's superior, to humiliate you

Sometimes it's a little syrup

When the cough is cured

here comes new flu

very strong half assail

He's wordy

To gain trust and revenge

He is a Fortunate man of envy

Kills silently, with his words

10 hours

April 21, 2021

The past

Suffering so much remembering
unrecorded and shared moments
unintentionally, in myself, to speak,
pick up on them clipped thoughts

go down on your knees on the floor
suffering to satisfy desires
surrender fate to forgiveness
the time was uneducated and made of miracles

The mind that is a school of rumours
revenge burning of the poor skin
the world was not made of favours
wise, they deny themselves, because they live in it

Joy of instincts

Smile, opened the chest
To read the lost joy
In the consciousness that was undertaken
Findings that would not irritate

Sleep took the time
They were things that arose from absences
Like measles, pranks
That appear by surprises

I know I never cried
But what's the point of crying in vain
If even crying I won't have
The hot sweat of thunder

A word can have several meanings

Like the silence that walks around me

Cause I'm afraid it'll surprise me with secrets

Embracing a stone of ice, I will never have the dear heat

October 25, 2015
18:36'

May be one day

May be one day

I will understand why demons

Are torturing me this way

Long hours and long dreams

Long feeling that can't be reached

Maybe the feeling to touch

Let the life goes on

to have an eye on

to be able to see the soul

hidden behind the desire

to quench the fire in you

I can feel am here for you

12/7/2022

Life is too short

Can't the sun shine twice

The wind can change any time

Live the moment that can't be learnt

More pain more lesson

That is the ethic of life

When I thought that has gone

I run inside me

Just to say yes in completions

For the hand blessed I was received

I'll need a guitar to sing

The moment that I loved

I will never forget madam

The time, the moment, environment

I touched and felt my heart

20 July, 2008

Confused

Nightmares come for everyone

When the dreams to become,comes

I feel insane and crazy

the fire of love comes

I deeply forget myself

shelter doesn't exist

only my ten fingers with me

where am I and where am I going

just madness, ideas flashing in my mind

morning is always a happy friend

always invite me to wake up

invite me to forget

invite me to prove my self

I'm really in trance

04.11.2022

Nothing to complain

Sunrise to sunset
Dream with brothers
Where can I find them
Dream with sisters
I am the only one left

Yesterday, in the land of sadness
Things are not as they should be
In the verse of life nothing can wait
Until the end of the road

I was born crazy
Everybody can see my soul
I have forgotten, I am deep inside

In my love there are two signs

Happiness across the sadness

The road is too small

We walk away just to gain

Push them to the wall

Waiting again and again

People get older

Things changes and life smiles

In the circle of age

We become again younger

Hear the voice of heaven

The only savior we can trust

22.11.2022

Sad verse

One can throw words at someone

It can be accepted or it can be refused.

Depending on the amount of pain

Expenses incurred with sadness

Are charged for the tears

In your innocence of situations

Come pages of lamentations

Forgiving that I was born

To cry in people's arms

Like the suffering that grew from life

let me in yeah

Cause they're just regrets

which is expensive

25.11.2022

Is for you baby

When I drown in loneliness

I carry the world on my shoulders

Sometimes nowhere to cry

Tears are firefighter's everyday

Along the way I have seen

Many blue hearts to have

But because I fear the dark

I become lonely man

Fear are sequels that

Are fallowing me in the past

I can say that is said

Nevertheless, I can lose the opportunity

I have been succumbed

Due to love frustrations

Without affective interaction

I decided to take my way

12 /12/2022

Distant world

Coming in the distant world

Where words hurt my wisdom

I live in a distant world

where carnal joy is denied

It's true in the hands of those who have the power

Begging for a crumb of love

Which has been never granted

Excuses come from everywhere

like refuge to denial

Even though I'm happy in the sadness

It's hard to fake your true appearance

because destiny is hidden

the distant world of my desires

for they were lost in the wrath of despair

distant world inside me

that makes me dream ahead

15.03.2024

Poetry world

When I lose strength

I forget the power of love

Lonely moments always hides

Feelings that I deceive to regret

Born in poetry world

Struggling for a crumb of love

Begging down on my knees

Just to gain a little value

Today I don't have a nose

To smell the loved flowers

But the flavor of being poet

Anyway, I have eyes to smile

There is always a sign

For those who have the power

The power of magic imagination

That make them poets

April 7, 2024

The walls of love

In beginning sounds good and cute

As times goes on

Water began to poison

There's a factory of lairs

Love of rough disputes

All wants to be the winners

A lot of excuses in their way

Just to cover the mistakes

Love

Is always a fire

That we feel everyday

Tears are the firefighters

In the moment of sadness

Love is a sunrise to sunset

Because you can feel the moment

Love is greatest desire

Is what make us feel to be alive

Love is inside paradise

You choose your own happiness

Love is having fever in your eyes

When you have an askance look

Love is eyes communications

Only poets understand

The proper time to react

Love is what you live everyday

2004

Mercy of love

There's always a sign

Seem as humble tough

Some tears contain

What can't see through

On the silence of the knees

Tears across the lovely chest

Begging for mercy of tears

The loved is the lost

Father! Forgive-me

I loved the world

Today is against me

Everything is left behind

A broken heart, of course

Is best healed good deed

Hardly left no excuse

For anyhow arise

Heart ablaze

Oh my God, I'm on fire
A burning pain in my chest
I traded feelings for madness
I was fooled beyond measure

Oh my God, give me light
To soften her heart
True love lasts longer
There's a door for forgiveness

Pride tortures me
It invaded my conscious
I'm on fire
Open the door for forgiveness

We're humans
We were in the adventure
Of calculating desire
Love always talks
2025

Matter of love

Looking the blue of sky

Too fine a blue heart

Random memories comes

To catch the destination

The hidden destinations

Is always a hard way

To capture the moment of feeling

That can be touched

The meaning of love

Is what he has been looking for?

Sleeping everyday sad

Working up happy

The mercy of sun

Shine to capture the lost feeling

The wind to captures your thoughts

Always has time to begin

Where is the reason

To be upset and alone

What is the thermostats of love?

How do you feel to be alive?

June, 2025

The other side of the love

Happiness always measures

The meaning of love

Feeling the sun shining

Is what is called love

Both are the chosen

For a long way destiny

A brilliant empathy

That will not be forgotten

The other side of love

Is always a lesson

To learn from mistakes

Where's love

Looking left and right

In tentative of finding luck

The moment you close the eyes

Moment that everything happen

Looking yourself as a looser

Because flowers are hard to smell

Everyday are flowers shining

But can't find mine

Crying, I say very little

Rivers of tears on the chest

Doesn't give me chance

But a good love is always behind the line

June 2025

Mmap New African Poets Series

If you have enjoyed *The Tear of an Ophan Child*, consider these other fine books in the **Mmap New African Poets Series** from *Mwanaka Media and Publishing:*

I Threw a Star in a Wine Glass by Fethi Sassi

Best New African Poets 2017 Anthology by Tendai R Mwanaka and Daniel Da Purificacao

Logbook Written by a Drifter by Tendai Rinos Mwanaka

Mad Bob Republic: Bloodlines, Bile and a Crying Child by Tendai Rinos Mwanaka

Zimbolicious Poetry Vol 1 by Tendai R Mwanaka and Edward Dzonze

Zimbolicious Poetry Vol 2 by Tendai R Mwanaka and Edward Dzonze

Zimbolicious: An Anthology of Zimbabwean Literature and Arts, Vol 3 by Tendai Mwanaka

Under The Steel Yoke by Jabulani Mzinyathi

Fly in a Beehive by Thato Tshukudu

Bounding for Light by Richard Mbuthia

Sentiments by Jackson Matimba

Best New African Poets 2018 Anthology by Tendai R Mwanaka and Nsah Mala

Words That Matter by Gerry Sikazwe

The Ungendered by Delia Watterson

Ghetto Symphony by Mandla Mavolwane

Sky for a Foreign Bird by Fethi Sassi

A Portrait of Defiance by Tendai Rinos Mwanaka

Zimbolicious: An Anthology of Zimbabwean Literature and Arts, Vol 4 by Tendai Mwanaka and Jabulani Mzinyathi

When Escape Becomes the only Lover by Tendai R Mwanaka

ويَسهَرُ اللَّيلُ عَلَى شَفَتي...وَالغَمَام by Fethi Sassi

A Letter to the President by Mbizo Chirasha

This is not a poem by Richard Inya

Pressed flowers by John Eppel

Righteous Indignation by Jabulani Mzinyathi:

Blooming Cactus by Mikateko Mbambo

Rhythm of Life by Olivia Ngozi Osouha

Travellers Gather Dust and Lust by Gabriel Awuah Mainoo

Chitungwiza Mushamukuru: An Anthology from Zimbabwe's Biggest Ghetto Town by Tendai Rinos Mwanaka

Zimbolicious: An Anthology of Zimbabwean Literature and Arts, Vol 5 by Tendai Mwanaka

Because Sadness is Beautiful? by Tanaka Chidora

Of Fresh Bloom and Smoke by Abigail George

Shades of Black by Edward Dzonze

Best New African Poets 2020 Anthology by Tendai Rinos Mwanaka, Lorna Telma Zita and Balddine Moussa

This Body is an Empty Vessel by Beaton Galafa

Between Places by Tendai Rinos Mwanaka

Best New African Poets 2021 Anthology by Tendai Rinos Mwanaka, Lorna Telma Zita and Balddine Moussa

Zimbolicious: An Anthology of Zimbabwean Literature and Arts, Vol 6 by Tendai Mwanaka and Chenjerai Mhondera

A Matter of Inclusion by Chad Norman

Keeping the Sun Secret by Mariel Awendit

سِجلٌ مَكتُوبٌ لتَائِه by Tendai Rinos Mwanaka

Ghetto Blues by Tendai Rinos Mwanaka

Zimbolicious: An Anthology of Zimbabwean Literature and Arts, Vol 7 by Tendai Rinos Mwanaka and Tanaka Chidora

Best New African Poets 2022 Anthology by Tendai Rinos Mwanaka and Helder Simbad

Dark Lines of History by Sithembele Isaac Xhegwana

a sky is falling by Nica Cornell

Death of a Statue by Samuel Chuma

Along the way by Jabulani Mzinyathi

Strides of Hope by Tawanda Chigavazira

Young Galaxies by Abigail George

Coming of Age by Gift Sakirai

Mother's Kitchen and Other Places by Antreka. M. Tladi

Best New African Poets 2023 Anthology by Tendai Rinos Mwanaka, Helder Simbad and Gerald Mpesse

Zimbolicious Anthology Vol 8 by Tendai Rinos Mwanaka and Mathew T Chikono

Broken Maps by Riak Marial Riak

Formless by Raïs Neza Boneza

Of poets, gods, ghosts. Irritants and storytellers by Tendai Rinos Mwanaka

Ethiopian Aliens by Clersidia Nzorozwa

In The Inferno by Jabulani Mzinyathi

Who Told You To Be God by Mariel Awendit

Nobody Loves Me by Abigail

The Stories of Stories by Nkwazi Mhango

Nhorido by Siphosami Ndlovu and Tinashe Chikumbo

Best New African Poets 10ʰ Anniversary: Selected English African Poets by Tendai Rinos Mwanaka

Best New African Poets 10ʰ Anniversary: Interviews and Reviews of African Poets by Tendai Rinos Mwanaka

Best New African Poets 10ʰ Anniversary: African Languages and Collaborations by Tendai Rinos Mwanaka

ANTOLOGIA DOS MELHORES "NOVOS" POETAS AFRICANOS 10º Aniversário: Poetas Africanos Da Língua Portuguesa Selecionados by Lorna Telma Zita and Tendai Rinos Mwanaka

ABRACADABRA, by Olivia Ngozi Osuoha

DES MEILLEURS "NOUVEAUX" POÈTES AFRICAINS

10ᵉ Anniversaire : Poètes africains d'expression française by Geraldin Mpesse and Tendai Rinos Mwanaka

Taurai Amai by Cosmas Tasvika Manhanhanha

Nhemeramutupo by Oscar Gwiriri

Ntombentle: Selected Poems by Sithembele Isaac Xhegwana

African Poetry Anthology: Chapbooks, Vol 1 by Tendai Rinos Mwanaka, Lorna Telma Zita and Helder Simbad

Juices Of The Forbidden Fruit by Tapuwa Tremor, Mapaike

Like The Starry Night Sky, by Obinna Chilekezi

The Stench by Jabulani Mzinyathi

www.ingramcontent.com/pod-product-compliance
Lightning Source LLC
Chambersburg PA
CBHW071009160426
43193CB00012B/1987